Contents

Acknowledgments

The publisher would like to thank the companies and organizations listed below for the use of their recipes and photographs in this publication.

California Dried Plum Board

The Hershey Company

McIlhenny Company (TABASCO® brand Pepper Sauce)

National Pork Board

Cheery Cheese Delights

Cheese Pinecones

2 cups (8 ounces) shredded Swiss cheese
½ cup (1 stick) butter, softened
3 tablespoons milk
2 tablespoons dry sherry or milk
⅛ teaspoon ground red pepper
1 cup finely chopped blanched almonds
¾ cup slivered blanched almonds
¾ cup sliced almonds
½ cup whole almonds
　 Fresh rosemary sprigs (optional)
　 Assorted crackers

1. Beat cheese, butter, milk, sherry and red pepper in medium bowl with electric mixer at low speed until smooth; stir in chopped almonds.

2. Divide mixture into 3 equal portions; shape each into tapered oval to resemble pinecone. Insert slivered, sliced or whole almonds into each cone (see photo). Cover; refrigerate 2 to 3 hours or until firm.

3. Arrange pine cones on cutting board or serving plate. Garnish with rosemary. Serve with crackers. *Makes 12 to 16 servings*

Nicole's Cheddar Crisps

1¾ cups all-purpose flour
½ cup yellow cornmeal
¾ teaspoon sugar
¾ teaspoon salt
½ teaspoon baking soda
½ cup (1 stick) butter
1½ cups (6 ounces) shredded sharp Cheddar cheese
½ cup cold water
2 tablespoons white vinegar
Coarsely ground black pepper

1. Combine flour, cornmeal, sugar, salt and baking soda in large bowl. Cut in butter with pastry blender or two knives until mixture resembles coarse crumbs. Stir in cheese, water and vinegar with fork until mixture forms soft dough. Wrap dough in plastic wrap; refrigerate 1 hour or freeze 30 minutes or until firm.*

2. Preheat oven to 375°F. Lightly grease two baking sheets. Divide dough into 4 pieces. Roll each piece into paper-thin circle, about 13 inches in diameter, on floured surface. Sprinkle with pepper; press firmly into dough.

3. Cut each circle into 8 wedges; place on prepared baking sheets. Bake 10 to 12 minutes or until crisp. Store in airtight container for up to 3 days. *Makes 32 crisps*

*Dough can be made in advance and frozen at this point. To prepare frozen dough, thaw in the refrigerator before proceeding as directed.

Peppery Brie en Croûte

2 (4-ounce) packages crescent roll dough
1 (8-ounce) wheel Brie cheese
2 tablespoons TABASCO® brand Green Jalapeño Pepper Sauce, divided
1 egg, beaten
Crackers

1. Preheat oven to 375°F. Work crescent roll dough into thin circle large enough to completely wrap cheese. Place cheese in center of dough circle. Prick top of cheese several times with fork. Slowly pour 1 tablespoon TABASCO® Green Sauce over top of cheese. Let stand briefly for sauce to sink in.

2. Add remaining 1 tablespoon TABASCO® Green Sauce, pricking cheese several more times with fork. (Some sauce will run over side of cheese.) Bring edges of dough over top of cheese, working it together to completely cover cheese. Brush edges with beaten egg and seal. Bake about 10 minutes, following directions on crescent roll package. (Do not overbake, as cheese will run.) Serve immediately with crackers. *Makes 8 to 10 servings*

Delicious Dips

Creamy Dill Veggie Dip

4 ounces cream cheese*
½ package dry ranch salad dressing mix (about 2 tablespoons)
2 tablespoons milk*
1½ teaspoons dried dill weed *or* 1 tablespoon chopped fresh dill
4 cups raw vegetables (such as cherry tomatoes, celery sticks, baby carrots, broccoli florets, cucumber slices, zucchini slices and/or red or green bell pepper strips)
8 unsalted breadsticks

Reduced-fat cream cheese and reduced-fat or fat-free (skim) milk can be substituted for regular.

1. Place cream cheese, dressing mix, milk and dill weed in blender or food processor; blend until smooth.

2. Serve immediately with vegetables and breadsticks or refrigerate in airtight container. *Makes 8 servings*

 Tip: For an attractive presentation, divide dip among individual cups or ramekins so guests can each have their own serving. Place in crushed ice to keep chilled, if desired. Also, you can double this recipe if necessary.

Oriental Salsa

1 cup diced unpeeled cucumber
½ cup thinly sliced green onions
½ cup chopped red bell pepper
⅓ cup coarsely chopped fresh cilantro
2 tablespoons reduced-sodium soy sauce
1 tablespoon rice vinegar
1 clove garlic, minced
½ teaspoon dark sesame oil
¼ teaspoon red pepper flakes
   Easy Wonton Chips (recipe follows) or assorted fresh vegetables

Combine cucumber, green onions, bell pepper, cilantro, soy sauce, vinegar, garlic, oil and red pepper flakes in medium bowl until well blended. Serve immediately with Easy Wonton Chips or refrigerate in airtight container. *Makes 4 servings*

Easy Wonton Chips

1 tablespoon reduced-sodium soy sauce
2 teaspoons peanut or vegetable oil
½ teaspoon sugar
¼ teaspoon garlic salt
12 wonton wrappers

1. Preheat oven to 375°F. Coat 15×10-inch jelly-roll pan with nonstick cooking spray. Combine soy sauce, oil, sugar and garlic salt in small bowl; mix well.

2. Cut each wonton wrapper diagonally in half. Place on prepared pan. Brush soy sauce mixture lightly over both sides of wrappers.

3. Bake 4 to 6 minutes or until crisp and lightly browned, turning after 3 minutes. Transfer to wire rack; cool completely.

Makes 2 dozen chips

Roasted Eggplant Dip

2 eggplants (about 1 pound each)
¼ cup lemon juice
3 tablespoons tahini*
4 cloves garlic, minced
2 teaspoons hot pepper sauce
½ teaspoon salt
1 tablespoon chopped fresh parsley (optional)
4 pita bread rounds, cut into quarters

Tahini is available in the ethnic section of the supermarket or in Middle Eastern grocery stores.

1. Prepare grill for direct cooking. Prick eggplants in several places with fork. Place eggplants on grid. Grill, covered, over medium-high heat 30 to 40 minutes or until skin is black and blistered and pulp is soft, turning often. Peel eggplants when cool enough to handle; discard skins. Let cool to room temperature.

2. Place eggplant pulp in food processor with lemon juice, tahini, garlic, pepper sauce and salt; process until smooth. Refrigerate at least 1 hour before serving to allow flavors to blend. Garnish with parsley. Serve with pita bread. *Makes 8 servings*

 Tip: You can prepare the eggplants in the oven instead, if you prefer. Preheat the oven to 400°F and place the eggplants on a baking sheet. Roast about 1 hour, turning once or twice, until the eggplants are soft. Proceed as directed above.

Three-Mushroom Ratatouille

1 package (3½ ounces) fresh shiitake mushrooms*
1 tablespoon olive oil
1 large onion, chopped
4 cloves garlic, minced
1 package (8 ounces) button mushrooms, chopped
1 package (6 ounces) cremini mushrooms, chopped
1 cup vegetable or chicken broth
½ cup chopped fresh tomato
2 tablespoons grated Parmesan cheese
2 tablespoons chopped fresh parsley
3 pita breads (6 inches each)

Or substitute 1 ounce dried black Chinese mushrooms. Place dried mushrooms in small bowl; cover with warm water. Soak 20 minutes to soften. Drain; squeeze out excess moisture. Prepare as directed in step 1.

1. Remove and discard stems from shiitake mushrooms; chop caps.

2. Heat oil in large skillet over medium heat. Add onion and garlic; cook and stir 5 minutes. Add mushrooms; cook and stir 5 minutes.

3. Add broth; bring to a boil. Cook about 10 minutes or until liquid is absorbed. Remove from heat. Stir in tomato, cheese and parsley. Spoon into bowl.

4. Preheat broiler. Split each pita bread horizontally in half. Stack halves; cut stack into 6 wedges. Arrange wedges in single layer on baking sheet. Broil 4 inches from heat 1 to 3 minutes or until wedges are toasted.

5. Arrange toasted pita bread triangles and warm dip on serving platter.   *Makes about 2¼ cups*

Savory Bites

Festive Franks

1 can (8 ounces) crescent roll dough
5½ teaspoons barbecue sauce
⅓ cup finely shredded sharp Cheddar cheese
8 hot dogs
¼ teaspoon poppy seeds (optional)
 Additional barbecue sauce (optional)

1. Preheat oven to 350°F. Lightly coat baking sheet with nonstick cooking spray.

2. Unroll dough on lightly floured surface. Cut each dough triangle in half lengthwise to form 2 triangles. Lightly spread barbecue sauce over each triangle. Sprinkle evenly with cheese.

3. Cut each hot dog in half; trim off rounded ends. Place one hot dog piece at large end of one dough triangle. Roll up jelly-roll style from wide end. Place point-side down on prepared baking sheet. Sprinkle with poppy seeds, if desired. Repeat with remaining dough and hot dog pieces.

4. Bake 13 minutes or until golden brown. Cool 1 to 2 minutes on baking sheet. Serve with additional barbecue sauce for dipping, if desired. *Makes 16 servings*

Mini Asparagus Quiches

8 stalks asparagus
3 eggs
¼ teaspoon salt
¼ teaspoon black pepper
1 unbaked 9-inch pie crust

1. Preheat oven to 300°F. Spray 20 mini (1¾-inch) muffin cups with nonstick cooking spray.

2. Trim asparagus; cut into thin diagonal slices or coarsely chop to make ½ cup. Bring 3 cups water to a boil in medium saucepan. Add asparagus; cook 2 minutes over medium heat. Drain and immediately rinse under cold water to stop cooking.

3. Whisk eggs, salt and pepper in medium bowl; stir in asparagus.

4. Roll out pie crust dough to 13-inch circle. Cut dough with 3-inch round biscuit cutter. Gather dough, reroll scraps and cut to make 20 circles. Press circles into prepared muffin cups. Fill cups with egg mixture.

5. Bake 30 minutes or until tops are lightly browned and toothpick inserted into centers comes out clean.   *Makes 20 mini quiches*

Mini Swiss Quiches: Prepare muffin cups as directed. Whisk together 4 eggs, ¼ teaspoon salt and ¼ teaspoon black pepper. Stir in ¾ cup shredded Swiss cheese. Make dough circles as directed in step 4; fill with egg mixture. Bake as directed.

Easy Sausage Empanadas

1 (15-ounce) package refrigerated pie crusts (2 crusts)
¼ pound bulk pork sausage
2 tablespoons finely chopped onion
⅛ teaspoon garlic powder
⅛ teaspoon ground cumin
⅛ teaspoon dried oregano
1 tablespoon chopped pimiento-stuffed green olives
1 tablespoon chopped raisins
1 egg, separated

1. Let pie crusts stand at room temperature for 20 minutes or according to package directions.

2. Crumble sausage into medium skillet. Add onion, garlic powder, cumin and oregano; cook over medium-high heat until sausage is no longer pink. Drain drippings. Stir in olives and raisins. Lightly beat egg yolk; stir into sausage mixture, mixing well.

3. Carefully unfold crusts. Cut into desired shapes using 3-inch cookie cutters. Place about 2 teaspoons sausage filling on half the cutouts. Top with remaining cutouts. (Or, use round cutter, top with sausage filling and fold dough over to create half-moon shape.) Moisten fingers with water and pinch dough to seal edges. Lightly beat egg white; gently brush over tops of empanadas.

4. Bake in 425°F oven 15 to 18 minutes or until golden brown.

Makes 12 appetizer servings

Favorite recipe from *National Pork Board*

Artichoke Crostini

1 jar (about 6 ounces) marinated artichoke hearts, drained and chopped
3 green onions, chopped
5 tablespoons grated Parmesan cheese, divided
2 tablespoons mayonnaise
12 slices French bread (½ inch thick)

1. Preheat broiler. Combine artichokes, green onions, 3 tablespoons cheese and mayonnaise in small bowl; mix well. Set aside.

2. Arrange bread slices on baking sheet. Broil 4 to 5 inches from heat 2 to 3 minutes on each side or until lightly browned.

3. Spread about 1 tablespoon artichoke mixture onto each bread slice; sprinkle evenly with remaining 2 tablespoons cheese. Broil 1 to 2 minutes or until cheese is melted and lightly browned.

Makes 12 crostini

Tip: For a holiday color theme, garnish crostini with chopped red bell pepper, if desired.

Yuletide Yummies

Let It Snow!

2 (9-inch) round cake layers*
1½ cups prepared white frosting
½ cup prepared chocolate frosting
   Assorted gumdrops
1 sugar ice cream cone, cut in half crosswise
   Red pull-apart licorice twists

Cake layers will be easier to handle and decorate if they are frozen first.

1. Trim tops of cake layers to level. Cut off small piece from one side of each cake layer to form flat edge (so cake layers will fit together at "neck" as shown). Place one layer near bottom of serving tray.

2. Draw pattern for snowman's head (with hat) on 9-inch circle of waxed paper. Cut out pattern and place on remaining cake layer. Cut head and hat with sharp knife.** Attach flat edge of cut-out to flat edge of larger cake layer with small amount of white frosting.

3. Frost hat with chocolate frosting. Frost remaining cake with white frosting. Add gumdrop eyes and buttons, tip of ice cream cone for nose and licorice hatband and scarf.   *Makes 16 to 18 servings*

**Use cake scraps to make cake bites. Crumble scraps, then stir in just enough frosting to mold mixture into balls. Roll in sprinkles or ground nuts, then chill before serving.*

Christmas Cookie Tree

2 packages (16 ounces each) refrigerated sugar cookie dough
2 to 3 tubes (4 ounces each) green decorating icing with tips
1 tube (about 4 ounces) yellow decorating icing
1 tube (about 4 ounces) red decorating icing

1. Let dough stand at room temperature 15 minutes. Preheat oven to 350°F. Line two cookie sheets with parchment paper.

2. Roll out one package of dough to ¼-inch thickness between sheets of parchment paper. Cut out 7-inch and 6½-inch* circles with sharp knife. Transfer to prepared cookie sheet. Wrap and refrigerate scraps.

3. Repeat with remaining package of dough, cutting out 6-inch and 5½-inch circles. Transfer to prepared cookie sheet. Bake 10 to 14 minutes or until edges are lightly browned. Cool on cookie sheets 2 minutes. Transfer parchment paper and cookies to wire racks; cool completely.

4. Repeat step 3, using scraps to make 8 more circles, each ½ inch smaller in diameter. Reduce baking time as circles get smaller.

5. To assemble, secure largest cookie to serving platter with icing. Using leaf tip and green icing, pipe leaves around outer edge of cookie. Place small amount of icing in center of cookie. Add next largest cookie and repeat, adding cookies largest to smallest.

6. Pipe garlands around tree with yellow icing. Pipe ornaments with red icing. Serve cookies individually by separating layers or cutting into pieces with serrated knife.   *Makes 12 to 15 servings*

*Use a compass to draw 12 circles, each one ½ inch smaller, on waxed paper; cut out and use as patterns to cut dough circles. For a free-form look, use various bowls, glasses and biscuit cutters to trace and cut out 12 graduated circles.

Reindeer Cupcakes

1 package (about 18 ounces) chocolate cake mix, plus ingredients
    to prepare mix
¼ cup (½ stick) butter, softened
4 cups powdered sugar
5 to 6 tablespoons brewed espresso or strong coffee, divided
½ cup semisweet chocolate chips, melted
1 teaspoon vanilla
    Dash salt
24 pretzel twists, broken in half
    Candy-coated chocolate pieces

1. Preheat oven to 350°F. Line 24 standard (2½-inch) muffin cups with paper baking cups.

2. Prepare cake mix according to package directions. Spoon batter into prepared muffin cups, filling two-thirds full. Bake 20 minutes or until toothpick inserted into centers comes out clean. Cool in pans 10 minutes. Remove to wire racks; cool completely.

3. Beat butter in large bowl with electric mixer at medium speed until creamy. Gradually add powdered sugar and 4 tablespoons espresso; beat until smooth. Add melted chocolate, vanilla and salt; beat until well blended. Add remaining espresso, 1 tablespoon at a time, until frosting is of desired spreading consistency.

4. Frost cupcakes. Decorate with pretzel pieces for antlers and chocolate pieces for face.   *Makes 24 cupcakes*

Gingerbread People

½ cup (1 stick) butter, softened
½ cup packed brown sugar
⅓ cup water
⅓ cup molasses
1 egg
4 cups all-purpose flour
2 teaspoons baking soda
1 teaspoon ground ginger
½ teaspoon ground allspice
½ teaspoon ground cinnamon
½ teaspoon ground cloves

1. Beat butter and brown sugar in large bowl with electric mixer at medium speed until creamy. Add water, molasses and egg; beat until blended. Add flour, baking soda, ginger, allspice, cinnamon and cloves; beat until well blended. Shape dough into disc; wrap tightly with plastic wrap. Refrigerate 2 hours or until firm.

2. Preheat oven to 350°F. Grease cookie sheets. Roll out dough on lightly floured surface with lightly floured rolling pin to ⅛-inch thickness. Cut out shapes with cookie cutter. Place cutouts 2 inches apart on prepared cookie sheets.

3. Bake 12 to 15 minutes or until set. Cool on cookie sheets 1 minute. Remove to wire racks; cool completely. Decorate as desired. Store in airtight containers. *Makes 4½ dozen cookies*

Sweet Table

Black Russian Truffles

8 ounces premium bittersweet chocolate, broken into pieces
¼ cup whipping cream
2 tablespoons butter
3½ tablespoons coffee-flavored liqueur
1½ tablespoons vodka
1 cup chopped toasted walnuts*

To toast walnuts, spread in single layer on ungreased baking sheet. Bake in preheated 350°F oven 8 to 10 minutes or until golden brown, stirring frequently.

1. Place chocolate in food processor; process until chopped.

2. Combine cream and butter in glass measuring cup. Microwave on HIGH 1½ minutes or until butter is melted and cream begins to boil.

3. With food processor running, pour hot cream mixture through feed tube; process until chocolate melts. Add liqueur and vodka; process until blended. Pour chocolate mixture into medium bowl; cover with plastic wrap and refrigerate overnight.

4. Shape chilled mixture into 1-inch balls. Roll in walnuts. Refrigerate in airtight container. *Makes about 2½ dozen truffles*

Brandy Truffles: Substitute 3½ tablespoons brandy for coffee-flavored liqueur and vodka; roll truffles in 1 cup powdered sugar.
Hazelnut Truffles: Substitute 3½ tablespoons hazelnut-flavored liqueur and 1½ tablespoons gold tequila for coffee-flavored liqueur and vodka; roll truffles in 1 cup chopped toasted hazelnuts.

Cheery Cheesecake Cookie Bars

1 package (4 ounces) HERSHEY₅S Unsweetened Chocolate Baking Bar, broken into pieces
1 cup (2 sticks) butter
2½ cups sugar, divided
4 eggs, divided
1 teaspoon vanilla extract
2 cups all-purpose flour
1 package (8 ounces) cream cheese, softened
1¾ cups (10-ounce package) HERSHEY₅S MINI KISSES® Brand Milk Chocolates, divided
½ cup chopped red or green maraschino cherries
½ teaspoon almond extract
Few drops red food color (optional)

1. Heat oven to 350°F. Grease 13×9×2-inch baking pan.

2. Place unsweetened chocolate and butter in large microwave-safe bowl. Microwave at MEDIUM (50%) 2 to 2½ minutes, stirring after each minute, until mixture is melted. Beat in 2 cups sugar, 3 eggs and vanilla until blended. Stir in flour; spread batter in prepared pan.

3. Beat cream cheese, remaining ½ cup sugar and remaining 1 egg; stir in 1¼ cups chocolate pieces, cherries, almond extract and red food color, if desired. Drop by spoonfuls over top of batter in pan.

4. Bake 35 to 40 minutes or just until set. Remove from oven; immediately sprinkle remaining ½ cup chocolates over top. Cool completely in pan on wire rack; cut into bars. Cover; refrigerate leftover bars.   *Makes 36 bars*

Scottish Shortbread

5 cups all-purpose flour
1 cup rice flour
2 cups (4 sticks) butter, softened
1 cup sugar

1. Preheat oven to 325°F. Sift flours into medium bowl.

2. Beat butter and sugar in large bowl with electric mixer until creamy. Mix in three-quarters of flour blend until mixture resembles fine crumbs. Stir in remaining flour by hand. Press dough firmly into ungreased 15×10-inch jelly-roll pan or two 9-inch fluted tart pans; crimp and flute edges of dough, if desired.

3. Bake 40 to 45 minutes or until light golden brown. Place pan on wire rack. Cut into bars or wedges while warm. Cool completely. Store in airtight containers.   *Makes about 4 dozen bars or 24 wedges*

Berry Good Dip

8 ounces strawberries (thaw if frozen)
4 ounces cream cheese, softened
¼ cup sour cream
1 tablespoon sugar
  Orange peel (optional)
  Assorted cut-up fresh fruit

1. Place strawberries in blender; process until smooth.

2. Beat cream cheese in small bowl until smooth. Stir in sour cream, strawberry purée and sugar until well blended. Cover and refrigerate.

3. To serve, spoon dip into serving bowl. Garnish with orange peel, if desired. Serve with fruit.   *Makes 6 servings*

Scottish Shortbread

Marbled Pumpkin Cheesecake Squares

¼ cup reduced-fat cream cheese, softened
2 tablespoons granulated sugar
3 tablespoons egg substitute
1 cup packed brown sugar
½ cup Dried Plum Purée (recipe follows) or dried plum butter
2 egg whites
1½ teaspoons vanilla
1 cup all-purpose flour
1 teaspoon baking powder
¾ teaspoon ground cinnamon
¼ teaspoon ground ginger
¼ teaspoon salt
⅛ teaspoon ground cloves
¾ cup canned pumpkin

Preheat oven to 350°F. Coat 8-inch square baking pan with vegetable cooking spray. In small bowl, beat cream cheese and granulated sugar until blended. Gradually add egg substitute, beating until blended. Set aside. In large bowl, beat brown sugar, dried plum purée, egg whites and vanilla until well blended. In medium bowl, combine flour, baking powder, cinnamon, ginger, salt and cloves; stir into brown sugar mixture until well blended. Beat in pumpkin. Spread batter evenly in prepared baking dish. Drop heaping tablespoonfuls of cream cheese mixture over batter. Using knife, gently swirl cream cheese mixture into batter. Bake in center of oven 25 to 30 minutes or until pick inserted into center comes out clean. Cool in baking dish 15 minutes. Cut into squares. Serve warm with fat-free vanilla ice cream or frozen yogurt, if desired. *Makes 9 servings*

Dried Plum Purée: Combine 1⅓ cups (8 ounces) pitted dried plums and 6 tablespoons hot water in food processor or blender. Pulse on and off until dried plums are finely chopped and smooth. Refrigerate in covered container for up to 2 months. Makes 1 cup.

Favorite recipe from *California Dried Plum Board*

Triple-Layer Chocolate Mints

6 ounces semisweet chocolate, chopped
6 ounces white chocolate, chopped
1 teaspoon peppermint extract
6 ounces milk chocolate, chopped

1. Line 8-inch square pan with foil, leaving 1-inch overhang on sides.

2. Place semisweet chocolate in top of double boiler over simmering water. Stir until melted. Remove from heat. Spread onto bottom of prepared pan. Let stand until firm. (If not firm after 45 minutes, refrigerate 10 minutes.)

3. Melt white chocolate in clean double boiler; stir in peppermint extract. Spread over semisweet chocolate layer. Shake pan to spread evenly. Let stand 45 minutes or until set.

4. Melt milk chocolate in same double boiler. Spread over white chocolate layer. Shake pan to spread evenly. Let stand 45 minutes or until set.

5. Cut mints into 16 squares. Use foil to remove from pan. Place squares on cutting board. Cut each square diagonally into 2 triangles. If desired, cut in half again to make 64 small triangles. Refrigerate in airtight container.   *Makes 64 bite-size mints*

Festive Fudge

**3 cups (1½ packages, 11.5 ounces each) HERSHEY₅S Milk Chocolate
   Chips**
**1 can (14 ounces) sweetened condensed milk (not evaporated
   milk)**
   Dash salt
½ to 1 cup chopped nuts (optional)
1½ teaspoons vanilla extract

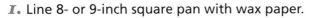

1. Line 8- or 9-inch square pan with wax paper.

2. Melt chocolate chips with sweetened condensed milk and salt
in heavy saucepan over low heat. Remove from heat; stir in nuts, if
desired, and vanilla. Spread evenly in prepared pan.

3. Refrigerate 2 hours or until firm. Turn fudge onto cutting board;
peel off paper and cut into squares. Store covered in refrigerator.

Makes about 2 pounds

Chocolate Peanut Butter Chip Glazed Fudge: Proceed as above;
stir in ⅔ cup REESE'S® Peanut Butter Chips in place of nuts. Melt 1 cup
REESE'S® Peanut Butter Chips with ½ cup whipping cream; stir until
thick and smooth. Spread over fudge.

Semi-Sweet Festive Fudge: Proceed as above using 3 cups
(1½ packages, 12 ounces each) HERSHEY₅S SPECIAL DARK Chocolate
Chips or HERSHEY₅S Semi-Sweet Chocolate Chips.

Praline Pecans and Cranberries

3½ cups pecan halves
¼ cup packed light brown sugar
¼ cup light corn syrup *Karo*
2 tablespoons butter
1 teaspoon vanilla
¼ teaspoon baking soda
1½ cups dried cranberries or cherries

1. Preheat oven to 250°F. Cover large baking sheet with heavy-duty foil; set aside. Grease 13×9-inch baking pan. Spread pecans in single layer in greased pan; set aside.

2. Combine brown sugar, corn syrup and butter in medium microwave-safe bowl. Microwave on HIGH 1 minute; stir. Microwave 30 seconds to 1 minute or until boiling rapidly. Carefully stir in vanilla and baking soda until well blended.* Drizzle evenly over pecans; stir until evenly coated.

3. Bake 1 hour, stirring every 20 minutes with wooden spoon. Immediately transfer to prepared baking sheet, spreading pecans evenly with lightly greased spatula. Cool completely.

4. Break clumps of pecans apart with wooden spoon. Combine pecans and cranberries in large bowl. Store in airtight container at room temperature up to 2 weeks. *Makes about 5 cups*

Add the vanilla and baking soda carefully because the syrup may boil up. Boiling sugar syrup can cause serious burns.